Pied Piper
A Hip Hop Family Musical

Conrad Murray

T0021661

methuen | drama

LONDON • NEW YORK • OXFORD • NEW DELHI • SYDNEY

METHUEN DRAMA
Bloomsbury Publishing Plc
50 Bedford Square, London, WC1B 3DP, UK
1385 Broadway, New York, NY 10018, USA
29 Earlsfort Terrace, Dublin 2, Ireland

BLOOMSBURY, METHUEN DRAMA and the Methuen
Drama logo are trademarks of Bloomsbury Publishing Plc

First published in Great Britain 2023

A catalogue record for this book is available from the British Library.

Library of Congress Control Number: 2023947482.

ISBN: PB: 978-1-3504-4890-2
ePDF: 978-1-3504-4891-9
eBook: 978-1-3504-4892-6

Series: Modern Plays

Typeset by Mark Heslington Ltd, Scarborough, North Yorkshire

To find out more about our authors and books visit
www.bloomsbury.com and sign up for our newsletters.

The BAC Beatbox Academy Presents:

Pied Piper: A Hip Hop Family Musical

Written, composed and musically directed by Conrad Murray, with written and musical contributions from the original cast.

Concept and story co-created by Conrad Murray and Lara Taylor.

Sally Snorekin – **Lakeisha Lynch-Stevens**
Pied Piper — **Conrad Murray**
Mayor of Hamelin – **David Bonnick Jr**
Crotchet —**Aziza Brown**
Solo – **Ananya Panwar**
Tempo/Simon – **Alex ('Apollo') Hardie**
Robyn – **Kate Donnachie**

Understudies – Celeste Denyer, Alexander ('ABH') Hackett
Community Chorus facilitators (at BAC) – Paul Cree and Native the Cr8ive

Direction by Conrad Murray and Ria Parry
Assistant direction by Amelia Thornber
Movement direction by Gavin Maxwell
Dramaturgy by Lisa Goldman
Set & lighting design by Ben Pacey
Costume design by Erin Guan
Sound design by Ed Clarke
rODIUM Ltd is produced by Impossible Producing
Producers Mary Osborn and Siobhàn McGrath
Comms (BAC) Sarah Fitzpatrick, Munaye Lichtenstein, Robbie Kings
PR Anna Goodman
Performance ethnography by Katie Beswick

This production was developed through workshops, with performance and devising by: Conrad Murray, Kate Donnachie, Lakeisha Lynch-Stevens, Apollo aka Alex Hardie, Ananya Panwar, Aziza Brown, Gambit Ace aka David Bonnick Jr, Renegrade, Tudor Davies, Jason York and Holly Race Roughan.

Commissioned by Battersea Arts Centre, Belgrade Theatre, Gulbenkian Arts Centre and ARCADE.

Pied Piper is supported by Arts Council England with additional funds from The Christina Smith Foundation, The John S Cohen Foundation, The Leche Trust, The Royal Victoria Hall Foundation and Youth Music.

BAC and rODIUM would also like to thank the following individuals for their generous support of *Pied Piper*: Eric Bensaude, Alison and Chris Cabot, Justin Shinebourne.

Thanks to our community chorus who were initially from the BAC Beatbox Academy: Woody Wyatt, Jacob Murray, Tyler (The Wiz-rd) Worthington, Isiah Wamala, Seth Stokes aka Beat-a-Max, Noah McGuiness-Smith, The Face, Duane Williams, Didiet, Foley, Shion, Pascal Blaschta, Luke Campana, Calley Otago Cole and Caine Cummings.

Special shout-outs go to Crown Lane Studio in Morden for the generosity, and to Liz Moreton for championing the BAC Beatbox Academy since the start.

Boom! Tee! Cla!

About the BAC Beatbox Academy

The BAC Beatbox Academy is a community youth music-theatre project based at the Battersea Arts Centre. Established in 2008, led by artist and director Conrad Murray with support from BAC producers, the Academy uses beatbox as a foundational tool, which provides a language for theatre-making. Participants take part in weekly workshops, which are free to attend and centre around developing beatbox and collaborative theatre-making skills through games and exercises. Members perform in productions developed with the Academy and can participate in the many external opportunities made available – these have included leading workshops in schools and theatres, appearing in commercials, and participating in professional theatre, film and television projects, among other opportunities. The group has maintained high weekly participation rates, with many members returning over a period of years, and has staged several successful productions, including 2018's *Frankenstein How to Make a Monster*, which received numerous awards, including an Off West End Award for best Gig Theatre production, and was adapted for television by BBC Four. *Pied Piper* is the Academy's latest show.

The Making of *Pied Piper*
Notes from the rehearsal process

Conrad Murray

I've led the BAC Beatbox Academy for fifteen years, creating songs, jams, games, scenes, sketches and shows. We have performed in youth centres, car parks, schools, universities, fetes, theatres, on the radio and in our very own BBC film. After creating our five-star hit, *Frankenstein* (which was the top-rated show at the Edinburgh Festival in 2018), we wanted to showcase more of what our young people can do, and push the envelope of what we had previously achieved. We decided to create a family show, which incorporated movement, characters and a narrative story. All whilst scoring the entire thing with only our beats. It would be a hip hop family musical. Plus, we wanted to incorporate a community chorus into the show. So, a bit of a challenge!

We started off by playing with some ideas at the Lyric Hammersmith, collaborating with their half-term theatre group – thirty kids running around as rebel clefs. Mental. Then BAC agreed to support the show.

Working on this show for the past few years, dealing with worldwide pandemics, funding disappointments and availability wasn't easy, but it has been a lot of fun. There have been changes along the way and everyone has fed into the process and the show's development. I'm really proud of the performance and the performers; in many ways we have already accomplished so much. The cast have improved their performance skills, lots of different performers have had the opportunity to be part of the process, and we've experimented with the whole BAC Beatbox Academy.

It has been great working alongside Ria and Gavin, two people that I have wanted to work with on a big project for a long time. Both have helped to elevate the characters and movement elements within the show and our wider practice, and I'm so excited to learn from both of them.

The story of *Pied Piper* shows how it only takes one person to spark the creativity and talents that we all individually have inside. Hopefully this show, through the workshops we do on tour and within the performances themselves, helps to spark that inspiration in people everywhere.

Enjoy the show!

You're welcome.

Katie Beswick

I've been fortunate enough to join *Pied Piper* as a performance ethnographer – which means that I've been asked to attend rehearsals, workshops and scratches over the past several years, keeping notes about how the play has developed (I've also helped to edit the script for publication). I first heard about this project when working with Conrad on our book *Making Hip Hop Theatre* during the pandemic. Following the success of their collaboration on the production *Frankenstein: How to Make a Monster*, Conrad and producer Lara Taylor had developed a concept for a children's hip hop show, based on the folk tale *The Pied Piper of Hamelin.*

Over the years of its development, the core story of a band of rebel child pie-factory workers standing against the tyrant mayor has stayed the same – but I've enjoyed seeing the play's story and staging change and adapt through workshops and BAC's signature 'scratch' process (where artists use feedback from audiences to improve their works-in-progress). Sally Snorekin, now a blogger working with the rebel clefs, was originally imagined as Hamelin's local newspaper reporter – and in an earlier version of the play, the rebel clefs escaped to a forest on the outskirts of town after the mayor banned all music, rendering Hamelin a silent city. I've also seen rehearsals where remote-controlled rats skittered about the stage (these were sadly later abandoned), and many BAC Beatbox Academy members join in with jams and devised compositions to create the production's distinctive musical world.

Like all BAC Beatbox Academy productions, *Pied Piper* is the result of collaboration. Conrad's words have been through a process of experimentation during workshops and cast members have contributed phrases and ideas later included in the final version. What looks effortless on stage is the outcome of years of hard work, belief and the trust and commitment of Conrad and Lara to developing their initial idea.

Ria Parry

I first met Conrad at Battersea Arts Centre when we worked together on his show *Denmarked.* It was a short rehearsal period, and we had plenty to do – but we still managed to find the time to chat in detail about politics, education and Wandsworth (where BAC is located and where I grew up). We got to know each other quickly, and connected in our belief that theatre should be for everyone – not just in relation to audiences, but makers too. And that it's always better to speak up than to complain quietly.

Conrad speaks with honesty, skill and style. It's a special thing working with a cast made up of alumni and current members of the BAC Beatbox Academy. There is a history and connection which fuels the company in a brilliant, beautiful way. And that is testament to the environment that's been created and nurtured over the years.

With his adaptation of *Pied Piper,* Conrad has taken a fairy-tale we think we know and blasted it open – for young people who want to chat about class, exploitation, and social injustice – for young people who love beatboxing and music – and for anyone – of any age – who wants to feel that theatre is for them.

Gavin Maxwell

As a movement director and theatre-maker deeply inspired by the world of hip hop, I was thrilled to be asked by Lara and Conrad to be involved in the creation of *Pied Piper*.

Saying yes to this production was an easy decision to make. Conrad, with his unmatched artistic vision, has proven time and again that he is a master of merging traditional storytelling with the vibrancy of hip hop culture. His previous production, *Frankenstein*, with the BAC Beatbox Academy, which I first saw at the Battersea Arts Centre and then later worked on as a movement consultant, showcased the Academy's ability to push boundaries and form and challenge conventions in theatre.

I wanted to be a small part of that on this show. I am thrilled at how this extraordinary production is not only a testament to the enduring power of hip hop culture, but also a beacon of creativity that transcends generational boundaries, making it an exhilarating experience for families and audiences of all ages.

Hip hop, with its five elements of emceeing, deejaying, graffiti art, (break)dancing and knowledge has always been a profound source of inspiration for me as a movement artist and theatre-maker. It's a genre that pulsates with raw energy and rhythm, offering a rich palette upon which to craft dynamic and expressive choreography. I feel this re-imagining of the Pied Piper story draws on these five elements both consciously and subconsciously throughout. The elements are present in multiple aspects of the production, including its design, artistic direction, choreography and incredible hooks, which I can guarantee will be stuck in your head for some time to come!

One of the most exhilarating aspects of *Pied Piper*, for me, has been the creative collaboration between Conrad and some of the UK's best beatboxers and singers. The synergy between movement and music has resulted in choreography that is playful and creative but also harmoniously synchronised with the captivating beats and rhythms of beatboxing. It's a testament to the incredible talent and dedication of the performers and a reminder of the boundless possibilities of artistic collaboration.

In *Pied Piper* you'll embark on a journey that celebrates the essence of hip hop culture, where storytelling is enriched by the rhythm of the streets, and movement is a language that transcends words.

The cast rehearse with BAC Beatbox Academy members, David Bonnick Jr as Mayor at the centre. Photo credit: Fettis films.

Ananya Panwar as solo, with Alex ('Apollo') Hardie as Tempo and Kate Donnachie as Robyn. Photo credit: Fettis films.

Lakeisha Lynch-Stevens as Sally Snorekin. Photo credit: Fettis films.

Conrad Murray as Pied Piper. Photo credit: Fettis films.

Pied Piper and Class in the City

By Katie Beswick

In the original folk story, which is believed to be based on a true event, Hamelin's children are lured away by a charismatic piper when the mayor refuses him payment for ridding the town of its rats. The 'Pied Piper' story has been told in many versions, from Grimm's fairy-tale to the famous Robert Browning poem, in which he described a vermin-infested Hamelin, where rats, 'fought the dogs and killed the cats/And bit the babies in the cradles/And ate the cheeses out of the vats/And licked the soup from the cooks' own ladles . . .'. In this BAC Beatbox Academy show, we visit a newly imagined 2023 version of Hamelin, where the main industry is a rat-infested pie factory in which the town's children work for a ruthless mayor. With few breaks and no appreciation for their graft, the children are forbidden from making noise or entertaining themselves during their shifts.

Fed up with being exploited, and desperate for entertainment, the children form a secret band called the rebel clefs whose activity is reported online by factory worker and blogger Sally Snorekin – who also makes vlogs about the town's growing rat problem. The mayor sets his young daughter, Robyn, to oversee the factory children and keep them in their place – but she is soon seduced by the rebel clefs' energy and the possibility of fulfilling her own dreams of making music by joining them. When the mayor offers one hundred guilders to whoever can rid the town of its rats, the Piper arrives, sparking a chain of events that leads to Robyn viewing the factory children as people rather than simply workers, with the mayor exposed as the town's real rat.

The workplace setting for this play might seem a strange change from existing versions of the tale, but by placing the story in a factory, Murray and the Academy make a wider point about class inequality in our current society. The term 'labour relations' refers to the unequal power relationship between workers and those who employ them. The theorist Karl Marx argued that groups who have access to the 'means of production' (that is the buildings, tools and resources to produce goods and services) have the most power, and can exert control over those who are reliant on the work provided by these means in order to live. This inequality in power is the bedrock of class inequality, which lays the foundations for all inequality in our society. In Hamelin, we see an imbalance of power between the mayor and the factory workers, between the mayor and his daughter, and a struggle for power between the mayor and the Pied Piper. The workers, meanwhile, tussle to find a sense of solidarity between themselves. In one way or another, these struggles can be understood as class struggles, with the worker-children representing society's working class, who the town of Hamelin come to understand they cannot function without.

The story of Hamelin therefore becomes, in this production, a wider comment on the class struggles of our society, and particularly of life in London, where the play was developed and first performed. In London, economic inequality is rife, with extreme wealth sitting alongside abject poverty. According to data collected by the London Mayor's office, the richest ten per cent of Londoners earn more than ten times the income of the lowest-earning households in the city. The UK government estimate that over 600,000 of London's children (that's about thirty-three per cent) are living in poverty, which means they exist in households that cannot afford to consistently provide the staples of life, such as food and shelter, or access necessities that make life easier, such as transport and childcare.

In this context, Pied Piper reminds us not just that society should be more equal, but that music and creativity can help us to access such equality. It is by seeing one another in all our humanity, and acting in empathy and solidarity, that we can begin to make cities fairer and life more joyful for everyone. That's a very humanist sentiment in these difficult times, emphasising the power not only of art, but of our relationships with each other, and the emotional ties that bond us.

Company Bios

Aziza Brown (Crotchet)

Aziza completed a foundation year in Acting at LAMDA. In 2022 she took part in BAC Beatbox Academy's UK tour of *Frankenstein*, which included performing at Regent's Park Open Air Theatre. She has represented the BAC Beatbox Academy on *Blue Peter* and on BBC Radio London.

David Bonnick Jr (aka Gambit Ace) (Mayor of Hamelin)

David Jr is an actor from south London. He trained at Mountview. Credits include: *EastEnders* (BBC); *Addicted to Love* (ITV); *The Day The Waters Came*, *Scratched Out*, *High Rise e(S)tate of Mind* (BAC); *The Making of a Monster* (Wales Millennium Centre). David Jr is also a rap artist and has recorded music that is streamed on all music services. He performs at gigs and music festivals such as Boomtown, Wilderness, iluvlive and other hip hop events.

Ed Clarke (Sound design)

Ed's previous work includes: *The Mysteries*, and *The Good Hope* (National Theatre), *The Wizard of Oz* (Royal Festival Hall), and *Bad Man Christmas* (HMP Wormwood Scrubs). He has been an associate designer for *Mary Poppins* (UK and US tours), *My Fair Lady* (UK and US tours) and has previously toured with Ryuichi Sakamoto, John Tams, Evelyn Glennie and Talvin Singh. And almost, but not quite, Amy Winehouse.

Celeste Denyer (Understudy)

Celeste is an actor, musician and singer-songwriter and a recent musical theatre graduate of the Italia Conti Academy of Theatre Arts. Previous training also includes: Mountview Academy of Theatre Arts and National Youth Theatre. Credits while training include *Carrie* (Margaret) and *Urine Town* (ensemble). Previous credits include: *Oliver!* (Theatre Royal Drury Lane) and *Carmina Burana* (Royal Albert Hall).

Kate Donnachie (Robyn)

Kate is an actor, singer and beatboxer from south London who graduated from Italia Conti as a Carlton Hobbs Bursary Award Runner-up and Alan Bates Award finalist. She has been part of the BAC Beatbox Academy since 2014, training, performing at various venues from the Royal Festival Hall to Latitude Festival and now facilitating the next generation of beatboxers. Theatre credits include: *Unexpected Twist* (Children's Theatre Partnership and Royal and Derngate Northampton co-production national tour), *Crongton Knights* (Pilot Theatre national tour)*, Frankenstein: How to Make a Monster* (BAC Beatbox Academy national tour), *3 Years, 1 Week & a Lemon Drizzle* with her actor/writer sister, Alexandra Donnachie (Underbelly, Edinburgh Festival), *Return to Elm House* (Battersea Arts Centre), *Aladdin* (Lyric Hammersmith, Best Supporting Artist in the UK Pantomime Awards).

Erin Guan (Costume design)

Erin is a London-based scenographer and interactive installation artist from China. Her work spans intercultural performances and minority voices. Her recent theatre projects include *Turandot* (The Opera Makers & Ellandar x Arcola Theatre), *The Apology* (New Earth Theatre x Arcola Theatre), *A Gig for Ghost* (Forty Five North x Soho Theatre Upstairs), *Pressure Drop* (Immediate Theatre), *Unchain Me* (Dreamthinkspeak x Brighton Festival), *Prayer for the Hungry Ghost* (Barbican Open Lab), *Foxes* (Defibrillator Theatre x Theatre 503), *Tokyo Rose* (Burnt Lemon Theatre). Her recent TV work includes costume design for *East Mode S2 with Nigel Ng* (Comedy Central x Channel 5).

Alexander Hackett (aka ABH) (Understudy)

ABH is a beatbox Champion with ten years of professional experience. His accolades include UK Beatbox Solo Champion (2019), UK Beatbox Solo Vice Champion (2016), UK Beatbox Tag Team Vice Champion (2014 and 2015), Toyota Feeling the Street finalist (2015), London Beatbox Champion (2015) and Birmingham Beatbox Champion (2015). His work includes collaborations with the medical sector (Vocal Beats), as a touring artist for Folk DanceRemixed and as a collaborator and international touring performer with the multi-award-winning show *Frankenstein: How to Make a Monster*.

Alex Hardie (aka Apollo) (Tempo/Simon)

Alex trained at The Urdang Academy. His most recent theatre performance was as 'Gaz' in the UK tour of *Unexpected Twist*. Alex has performed with multiple groups such as BAC Beatbox Academy, Get Gospel and The Gold Vocal Collective.

Lakeisha Lynch-Stevens (Sally Snorekin)

Lakeisha is an actor, author, theatre-maker and an associate artist of Beats & Elements, who has performed and created for many theatres, platforms and locations UK wide. She is hugely inspired by the crossed wires between theatre making and music and by finding the most unique ways to illuminate complex stories. Lakeisha is the director of Camden Youth Theatre, a Jenny Harris Award nominee and has tutored and directed shows at Mountview, LAMDA, Arts Ed and Central. Credits include *High Rise eState of Mind* (BAC published by Methuen), *The Fellowship Project* (The Working Party) and *Birthday Wish* (British Urban Film Festival).

Gavin Maxwell (Movement direction)

Gavin is a neurodivergent theatre-maker and movement director and is the co-artistic director of GymJam Theatre. For GymJam, Gavin co-directed the company's OFFIE-winning choose your own adventure film *Anthropocene: The Human Era*, a co-production with Oxford Playhouse. He is a graduate of the East 15 Contemporary Theatre course and holds an MA in Collaborative Theatre Making from Coventry University. Gavin has worked as a practitioner for Frantic Assembly for over five years, sharing the Frantic method of devising all over the UK and the world. In addition, Gavin has co-directed the company's flagship outreach project Ignition in 2019 and 2022. He was an associate director of Frantic's 2021 production *I Think We Are Alone*.

Ben Pacey (Design and lighting design)

Ben has designed, lit, created and collaborated with lots of amazing artists and performers. Previous collaborations have included Touretteshero, Verity Standen, Sue MacLaine, Secondhand Dance, Jamal Gerald, Sleepdogs, Javaad Alipoor, Melanie Wilson, Zest, Fuel and Brighton People's Theatre. His work has appeared in all kinds of places, including theatres, art galleries, tunnels, warehouses, shopping centres, wardrobes, gardens, the internet and a palace.

He's a director of Dens & Signals (for whom he wrote *Animals!*), and an associate artist of Coney (for whom he made *The Circus*).

Ananya Panwar (Solo)

Ananya is an artist, songwriter, storyteller and poet working towards sustainable social innovation and cultural exchange.

Ria Parry (Direction)

Ria is Director of The North Wall Arts Centre in Oxford. She is a director and a producer, and has produced four Fringe First Award-winning plays, most recently *Brown Boys Swim* by Karim Khan. Ria's recent directing work includes *A Gig for Ghosts* by Fran Bushe (Soho Theatre), *The Apology* by Kyo Choi (New Earth at The Arcola) and *Burnt Out in Biscuit Land* by Touretteshero (Co-director, national tour). She has directed at the Bush Theatre, Regent's Park Open Air Theatre, Unicorn Theatre, Southbank Centre, Salisbury Playhouse and Young Vic. Ria was previously a creative producer at Watford Palace Theatre and is an alumna of the National Theatre's Step Change Leadership Programme. She was awarded the Leverhulme Bursary for Emerging Directors in 2010, becoming resident director at the National Theatre Studio.

Conrad Murray (Pied Piper/Direction)

Conrad is a theatre-maker, director, musician, writer and composer. As artistic director, he has led the BAC Beatbox Academy since 2008, innovating in hop hop/beatbox theatre with various projects. He was recently the musical director and composer on Roy Williams' adaptation of Michael Rosen's *An Unexpected Twist.* His production with the BAC Beatbox Academy, *Frankenstein: How to Make a Monster,* won the Off West End award, Total Theatre Award and 'pick of the fringe' at the Adelaide Fringe Festival. It was adapted into a BBC film in 2020. He was musical director for Pilots' *Crongton Knights.* Current projects include – *Romeo & Juliet (put down the swords & pick up your mics)*, for Polka Theatre (2024). He was beatbox coach on Giles Terera's *The Meaning of Zong* for the Bristol Old Vic. He directed Connor Allen's autobiographical show, *The Making of a Monster*, for the Wales Millennium Centre. In 2022, his first published works were released by Bloomsbury/Methuen Drama, *Making Hip Hop Theatre* and *Beatbox & Elements – A Hip Hop Theatre Trilogy*.

Pied Piper

Characters

Sally Snorekin *(blogger, sharing all of Hamelin's inside news)*
Pied Piper
Mayor of Hamelin
Robyn *(the mayor's daughter)*
Simon *(the mayor's deputy)*

The rebel clefs:
Solo
Crotchet
Tempo

All cast members play the ensemble.

Preamble

The stage is bare, dressed only with costume rails stuffed with lavish costumes and a few chairs.

Conrad (*as himself*)
Welcome everyone!!! We are the BAC Beatbox Academy! Have we got any beatboxers in the audience? We'll all be beatboxers by the end of the show today!

Before we get started, let me introduce everyone . . . [*each character enters giving us a taste of their vocal skills, before* **Conrad** *introduces the basics of beatboxing, the call and response pattern 'boom! tee! cla!'*]

When I say 'kids up' – you say 'rats down'! ['*Kids up! Rat's down!' Call and response.*] You're going to need that later in the show so don't forget it!

Today, we're going to tell you the story of the Pied Piper. It's set in a place called Hamelin, bit downtrodden, seen better days . . . somewhere not unlike Battersea.

And they've got a terrible rat problem. Hold onto your snacks.

The play takes place across several locations – a change in location indicates a change of scene.

Scene One

Location: Hamelin Town Square

Ensemble *as townspeople – they panic as rats begin to appear.*

RAT-A-TAT

Ensemble
Rats are everywhere! Rat a tat (x4)

Sally Snorekin
Rats in the kitchen. Rats in the sink.
Rats on the windows. Rats in your drink.

Even to close your eyes and just blink –
You run the risk of more rats moving in.
Rats in the kitchen. Rats in the sink.
Rats on the windows. Rats in your drink.
Even to close your eyes and just blink –
You run the risk of more rats!

Ensemble
Rats are everywhere! Rat a tat (x4)

WELCOME TO HAMELIN

Pied Piper
Welcome to Hamelin
Where once upon a time
Anything could happen
A nation so great
But the vision has faded
The colours are jaded

Welcome to Hamelin
Where back in the day
Had feeling and passion
So misunderstood
It looks good from far
But far from good

It's a town that looks like yours
Streetlights
Stray cats
Front doors
But the kids here work every day
For next to no pay
All sweat no play
They work in a factory of pies
Some say factory of lies
And it's just as bad for mum and dad
But the mayor reassures them

Mayor

It's the best they've ever had

Piper

In Hamelin
So proud they stand in old clothes
And sing the town's anthem so loud

Ensemble

We pledge with pride to the pastry
Bake every day, make sure that they're tasty!
Even if we don't got no dough
We will go we will go we will go
Till we can't cook no more

Piper

They make so much waste from the pies
And the cakes
The streets are crust-filled
Plus kidney and steak
Rats have filled the floors
Because of the state of the place
The mayor must know
Make no mistakes

Welcome to Hamelin
Where once upon a time
Anything could happen
A nation so great
But the vision has faded
The colours are jaded

Welcome to Hamelin
Where back in the day
Had feeling and passion
So misunderstood
It looks good from far
But far from good

We see one of the rebel clefs, **Crochet**, *on her own, deftly making pies.*

Crochet
> I'm gonna show this town
> I can put it down
> I can put it down

Scene Two

Location: The Pie Factory

The town's kids are miserably working on the pie factory production line. A rat bothers them every now and then. The **Mayor** *walks up and down, inspecting the production line, and then goes out of sight.*

GET NO CHILL

Announcement
> Bing bong bing! No talking, on the factory floor. Bing!

Factory soundscape begins. Each performer builds an element of the sound by vocalising machinery.

Announcement
> Bing bong bing! If you see a rat . . .

Sound cuts.

> Please do not feed it. Bing!

Factory soundscape resumes.

Announcement
> Bing bong bing! Your welfare is important to us, that's
> why we guarantee you a seven-minute lunch break.

Solo
> Only seven minutes to eat lunch?!
>
> I'm sick of working here
> I'm sick of working here
> I don't get no chill
> What a situation

No appreciation
Stuck in this location

Work every day on these dumb pies
I just wanna get away
But I never dare to try
We're supposed to be a group of rebels
But we never get into trouble
Crochet keeps making so many pies
But I'd wish she'd stop it
Showing off to the boss
But it's just your loss
You think that it's gonna help you
But no!
So stop showing off

Crochet
I'm sick of working here
I don't get no chill
What a situation
No appreciation
Stuck in this location
I'm sick of working here
I don't get no chill
What a situation
No appreciation
Stuck in this location.

Nobody knows all the facts
I come from the other side of the tracks
I live side by side with the rats
All the hustlers
Window panes with the cracks
That's why we use the music
Makes us feel like I can do it
I just wanna get on
Make my money
And go on home

Solo
>In this life you choose
>If you win or lose
>So why give your soul
>To a hopeless goal

Sally Snorekin
>Hey guys!
>It's Sally here!
>Make sure you all subscribe!
>Bringing you the gossip
>The hot tea
>Vibes
>Straight from me and my rebel clef guys
>I work at the factory
>You can see inside
>We're working hard but long gone
>Is our pride
>I'll tell you the truth
>I'll give you the flow
>If you like what you see,
>Comment below

Crochet
>I'm sick of working here
>I don't get no chill
>What a situation
>No appreciation
>Stuck in this location
>I'm sick of working here
>I don't get no chill
>What a situation
>No appreciation
>Stuck in this location . . .

The **Mayor** *comes in – sound cuts out.*

Mayor
>QUUUIIIIET!

Stop making music
Start mixing pies
No tapping
No clapping
Or humming
Or hawing
No squeaks
No squeals
No coughing
No snoring
Get TO WOOOORK!

He slaps the pies out of **Crochet***'s hand, leaving her sad and humiliated.*

Tempo *does the sickest beatbox solo, which shows how angry and stressed and annoyed he is.*

Solo
   Hmmm. He's not happy!

Solo *looks over to* **Crochet** *and is sad for her.* **Crochet** *really believes in the saying 'hard work pays off'. Maybe once upon a time it did, but not now.*

REBEL CLEF ANTHEM

Solo
   Kids don't got to be making pies (x4)

   You work every day
   You don't get no rest
   You are proud of your flans
   They taste the best
   I'm Solo
   I haven't needed no one to follow
   For so long
   Everybody's been so shallow
   Maybe, we can be the change
   That we want to see

We can't keep going on
We been doing this for so long
Rebel clefs/rebel clefs
Let's do what we're meant to do
Rebel clefs/rebel clefs
Let's do what we're meant to do

Kids don't got to be making pies (x4)

Crochet
I worked so hard for nothing extra

Solo
That's all because you were being extra!

Crochet
You know!!
No more let's kick out the door!

Tempo
And make no money!
What good's that for?

Crochet
I wanted to be perfect
I was the pie-fect
And for that what do I get?
Nothing after years of stuffing
Pasties an' pastries
All of them cakeys
Waste up my time!
At pie of the year,
The mayor always wins it
But we make the pie
So let's put rats in it!
So let's put rats in it!
Rats in the pie!

Rats in the pie!

Rebel clefs/rebel clefs
You know just what to do

Rebel clefs/rebel clefs
You know just what to do
Kid don't got to be making pies (x4)

Cheering.

The **Mayor** *opens his office door. The music stops abruptly. He shuts the office door. The jam continues. He opens the door again. They pretend to work . . .*

The **Mayor** *walks in and cuts them off mid flow. Silence! He calls on his daughter* **Robyn** *to watch them.*

Robyn *points to different stations of the factory, indicating where the kids should go to work. They shake their heads and refuse to move. She shows them dirt that she wants them to clean. They ignore her. As this continues, she becomes increasingly reluctant to order them about.*

YOU WOULDN'T KNOW

Crochet
   You wouldn't know
   Just how we grow
   Where it's always cold
   And the people don't go
   You might not have it easy
   But it's not the same as me
   Is there a chance that you
   Could understand?

How could she?

You'll think you can
Understand
Just why I'm stressed
And why I'm not
Hashtag blessed
It's not the same for you
I don't claim to understand it all too
But do you think

You know what I've been through?
How could you?

Robyn
I wanna sing . . . (*Chokes.*)

Laughter from all the **rebel clefs**.

Rebel clefs
Kids don't got to be making pies!
Kids don't got to be making pies!
Rebel clefs/rebel clefs
Gon do what we have to do!

Crochet *looks over at an embarrassed* **Robyn***, walks over to her, moves as if to punch her, and bumps fists instead.* **Robyn** *is happy; she has made a friend, despite who her dad is.*

Scene Three

Location: Online

SALLY'S VLOG

Sally Snorekin
Sally Snorekin!
I'm checkin in,
It's a mad ting
Tea – hot off the press
That Crotchet the hot head
Was talking to the mayor's daughter
I heard everything she said
Top news!
I saw the clues
Through the chit chat
I got the facts
It was not an act
Nor a pact
But they seem to be friends

Now they friends!
Solo don't like it but they seem to be friends
Now they are friends!

Scene Four

Location: Mayor's Office

MAYOR & HIS DEPUTY

Simon
Wow! So we are really on top of this rat problem huh?

Mayor
What? Are you crazy man?!
Do you really think
We have the better of these rodents?
Have you been watching the news?
The tweets? Word on the streets?
The papers/ the nosey curtain-bashing next door
neighbours?
Rats everywhere
They're probably having fun

The **Mayor** *goes to sit down, and then jumps up with a shriek.*

Music cuts.

Simon
Was that a rat up your bum?

Mayor
Watch it Simon!

I'm concerned about the rats
Maybe I'll flood Hamelin with cats?

Simon
That won't work.
We tried that in January

Mayor

Stop talking back to me!
Want to win pie of the year!
But what if the rats start flooding the
Factory!?
I wanna win, and I wanna win clear
I'll just say whatever they want to hear!
If hype won't work
Who knows what will?

Simon

I got a rat in my pants

Mayor

You're making me ill

Simon

Look sir!
They're making off with the cheese

Mayor

They'll take anything fool
And they'll take it with ease!
They'll eat your doughnut
Even the hole

Simon

What?

Mayor

Don't you know?

Music cuts.

A rat will eat anything!!

Music in.

Dramatic lighting change! Disco ball lights up the room. The
Mayor *pulls a sparkly mic from his drawer and takes his jacket off,*
he turns his waistcoat inside out to reveal a new, glittery waistcoat.

A RAT WILL EAT ANYTHING

Mayor

A rat will eat anything, anything, anything
A rat will eat anything, anything, anything

Sometimes they eat cheese
Sometimes they eat bread
They even eat the tiny crumbs that fall under the bed
They eat jelly
AH!
They eat egg!
AH!
They eat peas
And stinky old brie

A rat will eat anything, anything, anything
A rat will eat anything, anything, anything

A rat will eat pear
A rat will eat poo
They'll eat the bubble gum which sticks right underneath
your shoe
They eat jelly
AH!
They eat egg!
AH!
They eat peas
And stinky old brie

A rat will eat anything, anything, anything
A rat will eat anything, anything, anything

Mayor

A rat will eat anything, anything, anything

Tempo

A rat will eat anything, anything, anything

Solo

A rat will eat anything

Mayor

A rat will eat anything, anything, anything

Beatbox solo from each rebel clef.

Mayor *vamps:*

Ok kids, I need you to help me! What else does a rat eat
. . .?

A rat will eat – *audience suggestion*
A rat will eat – *audience suggestion*
A rat will eat – *audience suggestion*
A rat will eat – *audience suggestion*

A rat will eat – *audience suggestion*
A rat will eat – *audience suggestion*
A rat will eat – *audience suggestion*
A rat will eat – *audience suggestion*

Mayor *vamps.*

Ok, let's take it to the break!

Dance break.

A rat'll eat, rat'll eat, a rat'll eat
A rat'll eat, rat'll eat, a rat'll eat
A rat'll eat, rat'll eat, a rat'll eat
A rat'll eat, rat'll eat, a rat'll eat

A rat will eat anythiiiiinnggggg!!!!

Scene Five

Location: Hamelin Town Square

It is Hamelin's annual pie competition and everyone is gathered.

PIE IN THE SKY

Mayor
I'm a winner I'm a winner
Call me the king baker
Amongst all these fakers

Come against me
That's pie in the sky man
Gonna win this
I don't have to try man

Sally Snorekin
It's the annual pie competition
Everybody wants to gather round
And watch and listen
As he plays his position
As he stands by the pies
That he never baked
Biggest mistake
In his life

Solo
Nobody's clocking
Not even Robyn
So keep on putting em in
Every single year
We're sick of watching him win
Watching him drool
Now we're standing here watching the fool
Putting rats in the pies
Right in front of his eyes

Crochet
It's finally time
He's really gonna get caught out on
All of his crimes
When they open they eyes
They gonna finally see
The harsh truth of the reality

Sally Snorekin
The mayor wails
As he sees a patty
Full of tails
The crowd boos
As their king fails

Mayor

I can't believe this
Mischievous deeds
Have done me in
Rebel clefs!
I should put them all to their deaths!
Everything that I have done!
I should flambée them, every one!
Get in the factory!
Now!
Robyn! Tell me who did this
So I can stop him
You were watching them
You must have seen this traitor
Plotting

Robyn

Dad don't be mad
These are the best friends
That I've ever really had
My team, my squad

Mayor

Good God!

Robyn

Crotchet's had it bad
And she told me 'bout south Hamelin
There's more rats there
If you heard her story you would care

Mayor

I've had it!
We're nothing like them don't you get it??
No pay for the workers for a week!
I'll up the rent for the rebel clefs for a month!
Crotchet I'll have her sleeping in the
Streets like she was her mum!
And Hamelin
I hope you've all had your fun!

Cos if you found it hard
In the past believe me
That's gonna seem easy!
You're gonna get taxed
To pay for my prize loss
You're in this together
To make up the cost!

Robyn

If you put Crotchet out in the cold
You're placing her in the plague
It's swarmed with rats,
It's only safe in the day
She won't be able to find a home
Time's ticking away
Dad where will she stay?

Mayor

Whatever happens we are winners
Call us the town bakers
They'll never take us
Come against us
That's pie in the sky man
Challenging me
And I don't know why, damn

The **Mayor** *puts his arm around* **Robyn**, *who is disgusted with her father's actions, and embarrassed to be seen as part of his family.*

Crochet

You wouldn't know . . . You wouldn't know . . . How could you??

Robyn *is ashamed, as she accidently named* **Crochet** *as one of the culprits of putting rats in his competition pie.*

The **Mayor** *and his lackeys evict* **Crochet** *from her house, throwing her belongings into the street.*

Scene Six

Location: Mayor's Office

*The **Mayor** is desperate, fearing that his people will turn on him after losing the contest. He needs to hatch a plan to make them forget about his actions – losing and turning on the workers and children of the factory. He calls a press conference with an important announcement.*

*The people of the town all gather in, to hear the **Mayor***'s speech. They come from all sides of Hamelin.*

THE PRESS CONFERENCE (100 Gold)

Mayor
Order please, order please – take your seats.
Let's begin this press conference.
You've watched the pie-fest run
I got pie on my face
What? You think I am done?
In the pie charts – look over here
Pie of the year
How you would cheer!
But listen up
There may be rats
Who've chased the dogs
And scared the cats
And had their fun
And scratched your bums
But I got a plan for that
A great plan
For that

I'm gonna give gold
100 gold
To anyone who can run
These rodents out of town
By any means shut em down
Gold! 100 gold!

To anyone who can run these rodents out of town,
By any means, shut em down!
What would you do with a 100? (x4) (*to audience*)

100 guilders to the man who deals with
All these rats
Driving me bats
That's a lot of lolly for all you wallies!
I mean loyal subjects

I'm gonna give gold
100 gold
To anyone who can run
These rodents out of town
By any means shut em down
Gold
100 gold
To anyone who can run
These rodents out of town
By any means shut em down

Order please, order please – take your seats
Let's redress this press conference
And finally defeat this rat nonsense
Take your photos press
I know you are all impressed
I was down in the polls
Because of the pie
I'm coming back strong
Cos I'm that guy!

Townspeople
He's gonna give gold
100 gold!
To anyone who can run these rodents out of town
By any means
Shut em down!

Townspeople
If I win gold
I'm gonna get glam

I'll buy a new outfit
I'll get a new man
If I win gold I'll get a new tan
If I win gold I'll get a new van

Get gold now
Cut them rats for gold now
Ring the mayor get gold now
Rodents are scared get gold now
Peak for the rats if we kill em with cats
Rats on road get told now
Rat boys dem betta know now
It's gonna go down!

Black out rats' eyes, rat sounds.

Sally Snorekin
Rats in the kitchen
Rats in the sink

Mayor
100 gold!

Holding iPhone in hand, live-streaming to her followers

Sally Snorekin
As Hamelin media heaps on praise
The townspeople
Are still dismayed
Some are cheering
They've been played
Some of them look lost

Sally Snorekin signing off!

Scene Seven

Location: Hamelin Town Square

COME AND HAVE A GO (if you think you're hard enough)

Ensemble
Come and have a go if you think you're hard enough!
We got a problem here
Everybody came but it got too rough
They're taking over here
They're taking over here

Sally Snorekin
467 townspeople, have all shown up at the scene.
457 townspeople, have all turned up with a dream.
The mayor has offered 100 gold to give one person for free
If they can rid the town of rats, then that's their money to keep
447 townspeople, with 100 different skills
437 townspeople, wanna pay their bills
The rats – in packs, with big sharp teeth –
Are they looking for meals?
Some cash, to axe, the big long tails –
Wonder who'll get the deal?

Ensemble
Come and have a go if you think you're hard enough
We got a problem here
Everybody came but it got too rough
They're taking over here

Tempo
Squeak, squeak, squeak they were scaring my mum
Woke from her sleep when they bit her on the tongue
These rats are pests! My idea to get rid of them . . .
Is to get a steam roller and flatten them
Splat, splat, splat – that's the sound of the rats

Hear me laughing hard as I'm rolling past
It's pretty evil, I'm getting gassed
Of being clear of the rats at last

Ensemble

Come and have a go if you think you're hard enough
We got a problem here
Everybody came but it got too rough
They're taking over here

Solo

I could get my cat, I could get my dog
If I get them together they could chase the little sods –
You gotta trust me, that's the plan!
I'm gonna get the guilders from the big boss man

Tempo

How about we paint the streets with jam?
And on top of that jam, we stick some ham
And the rats will come and feast on their find
And they'll get so fat that they'll all go blind
Then we jump out and croquet em out
Everyone's happy and we get a knock about!

Solo

How about . . . smack em with a bat plan

Tempo

Light a huge fire plan?

Solo

Flush em down the loo plan?

Tempo

Poison jelly

Solo

I'll do something smelly

Tempo

Freeze ray

Solo
Flame thrower

Tempo
Cannon balls

Solo
Hurricane

Tempo
Nuclear fission

Solo
At one point, I thought 'stick em in a prison'

Sally
Stick em in a prison?

Solo
Yeah just stick em in a prison

Sally
You heard it here first

Solo
Stick em in a prison

Sally
Stick em in a prison

All
Come and have a go if you think you're hard enough
We got a problem here
Everybody came but it got too rough
They're taking over here

Rats are everywhere, we hear loud rat sounds.

The townspeople are defeated, as their efforts have not been able to defeat the plague of rats at all.

RAT-A-TAT (reprise)

Sally Snorekin
Rats in the kitchen. Rats in the sink
Rats on the windows. Rats in your drink
Even to close your eyes and just blink –
You run the risk of more rats moving in
Rats in the kitchen. Rats in the sink
Rats on the windows. Rats in your drink
Even to close your eyes and just blink –
You run the risk of more rats –
First to report –
Catch that font on the board it's in
Big fat font – REWARD
You can – flip the button and record; Sally hashtags – who gets rewards?
You get dms, huge fat rewards
I get retweets, I'm Sally Snorekin
Influencing, now we're recording – crawling rats
Walking
Into bushes and floors
All born with claws
They've torn their way through doors
Rats in the kitchen. Rats in the sink
Rats on the windows. Rats in your drink
Even to close your eyes and just blink –
You run the risk of more rats moving in

Ensemble
Rats are everywhere! Rat a tat (x4)

Sally Snorekin
Rat a tat-tat. Tat-a-tat-tat tat-tat-tah (x4)

Big night –
Me and the rebel clefs crew and
My tweets on the rewarding find that –
Everyone wants that prize
And everyone wants that fame – them, gold over them pies

Un – till they spot a rat –
Then, everyone wants to hide
Rats in the toilet. Rats in the sink
Rats in your burger. Rats in your drink
Even to close your eyes and just blink –
You run the risk of more rats moving in
Rats in the toilet. Rats in the sink
Rats in your burger. Rats in your drink
Even to close your eyes and just blink –
You run the risk of more rats moving in

Pied Piper *enters.*

Pied Piper
I heard your call
I heard it all
I'll bring you hope
In just twelve notes

Solo
Everybody wants to see the man
Who sings the songs
Somehow he gets the children singing
Dancing all along
And they sing, sing along
and they roared

Pied Piper
Everybody say yeah! (Yeah!) *Audience participation.*
Everybody say yeah! (Yeah!)
Everybody say yeah! (Yeah!)
Everybody say yeah! (Yeah!)

I heard your call
I heard it all
I'll bring you hope
In just twelve notes

Crochet
I been looking for this all of my life
Maybe music could make it right

Could we help this man
He's made the people see
There's more than we could be

Robyn

This could be my time
I could write the rhyme
The moment I've been waiting for
My fight for more
I'm gonna sing my song
And it might be wrong
But there's a chance to change
To create the age
Of telling your story
Could rewrite my history
Defeat the rats
Claim the reward
Show my dad the power of my vocal cords

Mayor

You're deluded
Who do you think you are?
A scientist? I wish you were
You know nothing of rats
Have no plan of attack
Get back to the factory
Your work is satisfactory
Go
Hamelin is my town and I wear the crown

Crotchet
Everybody wants to see the man
Who sings the songs
Somehow he gets the children singing
Dancing all along
And they sing, sing along
and they roared

Pied Piper

I heard your call
I heard it all

I'll bring you hope
In just twelve notes

Robyn *joins in on the final harmony of the* **Piper**'s *song. They have made a connection,* **Robyn** *feels confident in her abilities and individuality.*

Robyn *slowly builds her confidence and starts to sing.*

I WANNA SING

Robyn
I wanna sing
Try and do anything
My heart desires

I wanna sing
Show I can do anything
My heart desires . . .
If only they'd listen
Ooh if only they'd listen oh

I've got a song inside of me
Just waiting to be freed
All of these words
Are fighting in my head

I wanna sing
Try and do anything
My heart desires
I wanna sing
Show I can do anything
My heart desires . . .
If only they'd listen
Ooh if only they'd listen ooh

I've been trapped and I've been lost
Singing to the silence
But I feel a melody
And I'll find my own key

And I will sing my song
Find where I belong
I know my voice is strong
I know my voice is strong

And I don't give a damn if no one likes it
I'm singing for my freedom
I'll take it any way I can

And I don't give a damn if I'm chased down
I'm singing for my freedom
I'll take it any way I can

Everybody wants to see the man
Who sings the songs
Somehow he gets the children singing
Dancing all along
And they sing, sing along
and they roared . . .

Crochet *joins in, singing with* **Robyn** *in harmony.*

I'm gonna sing
I can do anything
My heart desires
I'm gonna sing
I can do anything
My heart desires . . .
If only they'd listen
Ooh if only they'd listen

The **Piper** *is impressed with* **Robyn***'s singing and gives her a smile.*
Crochet *gives her a big hug –* **Robyn** *is finding her voice!*

FEED HER TO THE RATS

Mayor
This Crotchet girl
Caused me to fail
She has to learn
That she ain't no good

Let's kick her out of the house
Put her in with the poor
That's riddled with rats
They're bound to bite
She'll never last one night
Little girl goodbye
These kids are so soft
She's no loss
Drag her away, right away
Right now, not tomorrow
Do it today!
Feed her to the rats!
Goodbye, don't cry!

Crochet *is dragged away by the* **Mayor**'s *men.*

Scene Eight

Location: Mayor's Office

Pied Piper meets the Mayor

Piper
Hey Mr Mayor, Mr Man, homie, fam
I heard the call!
Use the twelve notes, the octave, the resonance

Mayor
How is this relevant?

Piper
The tapping of the high hat
The shuffle of the beats
You must have seen how it makes you move your feet

Mayor
What? Me? How obscene!

Piper
It's in your dreams, it's in everyone, every daughter, every
son

It's as natural as the sun
You can hear it in the rain
In love and pain
In playground games
You can feel it in your name
From the ice cream man, to the guy in the market
To the beep from the van, when reversing parking
Balloons popping and babies laughing

Mayor

You think music can do it?!
You're even more stupid than you look
You're probably a crook
That's usually the profession of fraudsters like you
Singers, artists, let me ask this –
Since when have songs put pies on the table?
Do beats put steak in the bake?
Maybe raps put icing on the cake
Ok mate if you can make rats go away –
I'll give you 100 gold!!

Piper

That's a deal!
But don't forget to pay the Piper

Mayor

Yes, all right!

Pied Piper

Don't forget to pay the Piper

Mayor

Stop babbling on though

Pied Piper

Don't forget to pay the Piper

Mayor

He's lost the plot

Pied Piper

Don't forget to pay the Piper

Mayor
    Idiot!

Scene Nine

Location: Central Hamelin

RUNNING OUT OF TIME

Robyn
    It's getting late and we can't wait
    It's cold outside
    And I'm scared for my best mate
    Her fate don't look too good
    She's homeless
    And it feels hopeless
    To talk to the mayor
    He may be my dad but he don't care
    Or maybe he just isn't aware
    Of the perils outside
    He's never been there
    Maybe he's never been scared
    Cos the sun never shines in south Hamelin
    It's dark, it's cold, bad things happen
    It's a scary place
    The head guy there
    Has a scowl on his face
    It's overcrowded
    Packed right in
    You might venture outside
    But then go back right in
    Gotta save Crotchet
    The rats'll bite you there
    Hopefully the Piper will stop it
    Running out of time
    Her life is on the line

All because of me
I wanna set her free

Pied Piper *makes a magical spell on the people in the town with his music, and draws out music from within them – including* **Crochet**. *(He also draws beats out of the audience.)*

Pied Piper
Something is missing here . . . it's you

Pied Piper *gestures* **Robyn** *to come forward.*

Pied Piper *pulls out a note from* **Robyn** *which silences everyone.*

Circle jam commences / recommences!

RAT JAM

Sally Snorekin
There were lanes of rats
Thin and fat – grey and black
Being dragged –
By the Piper in fact –
Hypnotised them – he actually did it!
The rats in the city were spinning
Poking their heads out toilet bowls and swimming
They were lifted away –
City gates – couldn't hold them in place
The Piper handled the plague
Every single rat in Hamelin levitating
Leaving traces
Blocks of plate cheese
All the faces
In Hamelin cheered
As the rats disappeared (The Piper made the rats
disappear)

The last rat is left squeaking on the stage and is scared away by a beatbox noise.

Scene Ten

Location: Online

RATS DEAD LIVESTREAM

Sally Snorekin
    Rats dead! Turned Hamelin's river bright red
    Droppin in the ocean choking
    Some tried to jump out
    But there's no hoping
    Rats dead! Turned Hamelin's river bright red
    Droppin in the ocean choking
    Some tried to jump out
    But there's no hoping

    The Piper made everyone's dreams come true
    But he made them rats screaming too
    And the man dem cheered
    But was kinda weird
    Cos they got buss up
    From the tunes by the man with the beard
    And magical voice powerful pipes
    I live-streamed the whole event
    I got a thousand likes
    Fifty smiles
    And an alien emoji
    Hopefully
    This is the end
    And the Piper leaves
    And we all made a friend

    Rats dead! Turned Hamelin's river bright red
    Droppin in the ocean choking,
    Some tried to jump out
    But there's no hoping
    Rats dead! Turned Hamelin's river bright red
    Droppin in the ocean choking,
    Some tried to jump out
    But there's no hoping

Scene Eleven

Location: Hamelin Town Square

CELEBRATION SONG

Solo

    It's a new day
    We celebrate like
    It's a party
    And it's gonna go off (the rails)

    Hurray! It's a celebrate – celebration
    For the population
    Hurray! We're coming together as one
    It's a celebration

    Finally the streets are clean
    There's air to breathe
    Get a break for a day
    Have a drink on me

    Spread the word, grab your mates
    We're gonna party
    Gonna vibe all night
    At the after after-party

    It's a new day
    We celebrate like
    It's a party
    And it's gonna go off (the rails)

    It's the RC gang
    Represent all my friends
    Stick it to the big man

Sally Snorekin

    Everyone in Hamelin grab some Maltesers
    Everyone in Hamelin – stand or put your knees up
    Everyone in Hamelin's hanging with the geezers
    Everyone in Hamelin's family – have a feast up

See how they've come from a few different streets
People have run in to move to the beat
Couple have come in confused but they're pleased
Mystery man leaves no clues on the scene

Tis the time where I need my phone
Tis the time to live feed from home
Tis the time where my sweets get thrown
On my head – I can't be alone
On my head – I can't be alone

Scene Twelve

Location: South Hamelin

Crochet *is saved, as the rats are no longer a threat in Hamelin –
especially in south Hamelin where it was riddled.*

GLOW

Crochet
  Thank god the rats are gone
  It's safer now for all
  Maybe not for me
  Out here in these streets

Robyn
  A friend's the one that gives you their last sweet
  You sit and watch your favourite shows on repeat

  I know I wasn't there
  When life became hard
  But now I'd help to heal your scars

  We never started great
  But turned it around
  But things have changed
  Cos I'm here now

My heart is your home
You won't be alone
Whenever I go
I'll still feel our glow

Crochet
A friend is the one who saves your seat at school
When you're feeling down they tell you they think you're
cool
And I see you're trying to make amends
I don't want our friendship to end
I feel the warmth from you
Between us I know
That you and I have found that glow

Robyn
My heart is your home
You won't be alone
Whenever I go
I'll still feel our glow
I'll still feel our glow

Scene Thirteen

Location: Mayor's Office

DID YOU FORGET ABOUT THE PIPER?

Mayor
It worked!

Pied Piper
Did you forget about the Piper!

Mayor
The rats are gone!

Pied Piper
You gotta pay the Piper!

Mayor
I'm gonna win Pie Factory of the Year!

Pied Piper
Did you forget about the Piper?

Mayor
What's this freak doing here?

Music cuts.

I knew this 100 gold was a good idea!

Music in.

Pied Piper
Ok Mayor you can see me standing here.

Mayor
What do you want? 100 just for a song?

Pied Piper
One chance Mr Mayor you don't have to do wrong
You've taken from me now I'll take from you
We had a deal

Mayor
No contract! Fake news!

Pied Piper
It's always the same with men like you

Mayor
What do you want?

Pied Piper
This is what I'm gonna do
I'll take the ships from the harbour

Mayor
We'll buy more!

Pied Piper
The shears from the barbers

Mayor
  We'll buy more!

Pied Piper
  The lights from the streets

Mayor
  We'll buy more

Pied Piper
  The shoes from your feet

Mayor
  I have UNLIMITED money!!!

Pied Piper
  I'm gonna take your future

Mayor
  Go on then! You mad man!

Pied Piper
  I'm gonna take your future

Mayor
  Silly musician

Pied Piper
  I'm gonna take your future

Mayor
  What you gonna do?

Pied Piper
  I'm gonna take the children . . .

Scene Fourteen

Location: Outskirts of Hamelin

KIDS EXODUS

Pied Piper
  I've travelled lands and I travelled seas
  I came to you offered honesty

That's not a way that you should to talk to me
You should cross my palm with some apologies
Step to the left, step to the right
Your future will be out of sight
Everybody's gonna follow me
You could've handled this quite easily
Dance

Sally Snorekin
The kids all swayed, the kids were raised, their parents
amazed – their parents afraid
They couldn't escape, as little as eight – as little as four –
I'm sad to report
They slid to their doors – away from their beds, away from
their floors
And onto the ledge
of window panes
The view was insane
It's hard to explain
They slithered like snakes
Their shoulders would shake
Like a routine dance – in a trance
They slither towards the Piper – dipping – forwards, the
Piper
Slither for – the Piper, will or forced – the Piper
Lined up
I watched, all of Hamelin's kids – in the middle of the
night
Form a pattern with their lips as they beatboxed in time
Fixed pattern in a line – couldn't shake it or fight it
Couldn't break it – parents frightened, fear heightened
It's a nightmare
What a scene, the dream is completed
A genius –
Piper could beatbox the beatless
And magic their knees –
The kids would be free, to follow the leader
Onto the streets

Mayor

> I'll pay up – 500 gold is yours!
> That's more than the pools or lottery draws

Pied Piper

> Too late now you've had your chances
> It's time to pay the Piper

Mayor

> 500 gold! I'm not kidding
> Stop that singing

Pied Piper

> Dance! Dance!
>
> You had your chance to pay my gold
> Now it's too late
> I've got them all

Mayor

> You think you're good?
> With all that you've done?
> You love yourself
> You don't care about anyone

Pied Piper

> Your eyes were on the pies
> Your pies were in the sky

Mayor

> Why? The children?
> Not my Robyn!

Pied Piper

> It's too late

Mayor

> Someone stop him!

Scene Fifteen

Location: Online

UNITED SOUND

Sally Snorekin
Hey! Thanks for checking in
If you like my makeup
There's a link in the description
The kids of Hamelin are marching on
With their hero
I'm the last one left
Couldn't really follow
Cos I'm kinda tone deaf
An that's probably why I'm not an official rebel clef

(*Speech.*) I need to try and wake them up. Omg. Kids will
you help me. I need you
To make a beat for me so I can . . . I can try to sing! Sally
Snorekin Singer!! Maybe
I'll get my own name . . . Sally Semibreve . . . (*to herself*) *I'm
getting carried away!*
Will you help me Hamelin? Will you help me to create
some music?

Sally *conducts the audience to do a beatbox rhythm.*

Ok . . . this could be MY time . . . this could be my rhyme

(**Sally** *sings.*)

I feel that we can come together in one voice
We've learned to follow
Now it's time to make a choice
I believe we can do this
We've been through this
Let's stand together
Just turn around
Let's hold our ground

Many voices singing
Make a united sound!!!

On the outskirts of Hamelin, **Crochet** *is stirring, but* **Sally** *can't see*
. . .

(*Talking.*) did it! I sang . . . but nothing

Sally *looks out of her window.*

They're close to the rocks
No one can stop it
Someone's woken up and turned around, wait it's
Crotchet!

Scene Sixteen

Location: The edge of a cliff

Freedom Is the Power To Stay

Crotchet
Solo's at the edge of the cliff
When I joined the rebel clefs
I made a pledge
That I would do it til my last breath
There's rock to her right
And sea to her left
It's only right
That we fight
This doesn't seem right!

Freedom is the power to love
The power to believe
Freedom's the power to leave
Freedom is the power to think
To find your way
Freedom is the power to stay!

Sally Snorekin
Solo's climbing high
I can barely watch
Crotchet starts to cry
This can't be goodbye
She's almost at the top
It looks like she won't stop

Rebel clefs
We are the rebel clefs
Say we are the rebel clefs!
We are the rebel clefs
Say we are the rebel clefs!

Sally Snorekin
But as she hears the sound
Of her rebel clefs
She turns around!

Crochet
Please don't go no further
You don't no longer need the Piper,
Solo sing your songs we need em
We need you, we need each other
Please don't hurt yourself
Listen to me solo!

Solo
What am I doing?
Where am I going?
Crotchet? My friend?
I can hear you through the music!

Crochet
Stop it now
Be careful you could still fall
And lose it all
Solo, come to me!

Solo
I'm not happy

Why should I leave?
Wake up get up kids!

Robyn *wakes up from the* **Piper**'s *trance.*

Let's go back to Hamelin
A town where anything *can* happen!
Cos of us!
We may be kids
But this is the place *we* live!
The Piper helped
But we don't have to follow
It's not his, it's all of our tomorrow!
Let's take down the mayor
He's only there because of us
Let's kick him out of the factory
And run it ourselves happily

Freedom is the power to love
The power to believe
Freedom's the power to leave
Freedom is the power to think
To find your way
Freedom is the power to stay!
Freedom's the power to find your way

Scene Seventeen

Location: Hamelin Town Square

The townspeople turn on the **Mayor**, *as they realise that he is the real rat!*

THE *REAL* RAT

Tempo
You were so crooked
Told so many lies
We couldn't see

Now we've opened our eyes
We gave you the power
It went to your head
Supposed to be for us
You were selfish instead

Robyn

The people believed in you
It was too good to be true
Everything you put them through
It's a fact you are the real rat!
It's a fact he is the real rat

Tempo

You were our leader
You couldn't lead
You kept on taking
We were in need

Robyn

You made us think you cared
You made us feel aware
But the truth was standing there!

It's a fact
You are the real rat
It's a fact!
He is the real rat!
He is the real . . .

Crochet *and* **Robyn** *come together in an embrace after the* **Mayor** *is confronted, both realising that everyone has been a victim of the tyrant mayor.*

The town has turned against the mayor

The **Mayor** *is forced to stand down, which immediately creates a re election process.*

VOTING BATTLE

A beatbox/rap freestyle battle between characters.

Piper

And in the new tradition of Hamelin, where music, and
art, and people of all ages and backgrounds are respected,
the new mayor will be elected via a Beatbox Battle!
So – who tell me – who's battling the mayor for the top
spot tonight
Give me a cheer if you want to see Sally battle!
Give me a cheer if you want to see Crotchet battle!
Give me a cheer if you want to see Tempo battle!
Give me a cheer if you want to see Solo battle!
Give me a cheer if you want to see Robyn battle!
Which of *you* wants to battle?!?

Alright! Hamelin, tonight, in the grand mayor 2023
smackdown
We have XXX vs XXX for Mayor of Hamelin!

Ok, XXX, you going first? You ready?

3, 2, 1 –

3, 2, 1 –

Give me a cheer if you think X won, give me a cheer if you
think X won . . .
Hamelin you have spoken!!! Your new mayor is XXX!!!
Yes!!!

Winner

And my first orders as Mayor are
No kids in the factory
No kid ever has to work again!
Kids are gonna play!
And kids are going to make muuuussiiicc!!

KIDS UP RATS DOWN!

Ensemble
We've got the vibe right now
Nobody can stop us

KIDS UP RATS DOWN!

The music's back in town
We're gonna cause a ruckus

KIDS UP RATS DOWN!

We will sing our song
People come along
Together we are strong
Together we are strong

We don't give a damn if you want silence
We got the beat inside us
We'll sing it anyway we can

We don't give a damn if you want silence
We got the beat inside us
We'll sing it anyway we can

KIDS UP RATS DOWN! (x4)

The Piper's in town

We can feel the groove
Now the bass is thumping

KIDS UP RATS DOWN!

Because the march is on
A brighter day is coming

KIDS UP RATS DOWN!

We will sing our song
People come along
Together we are strong
Together we are strong

We don't give a damn if you want silence
We got the beat inside us
We'll sing it anyway we can

KIDS UP RATS DOWN! (x4)

The Piper's left town.

The End.